# What Is a Solid?

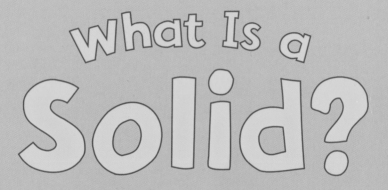

by Jennifer Boothroyd

first step nonfiction

Lerner Publications Company · Minneapolis

All things are made of **matter.**

Matter is anything that takes up space.

There are three kinds of matter.

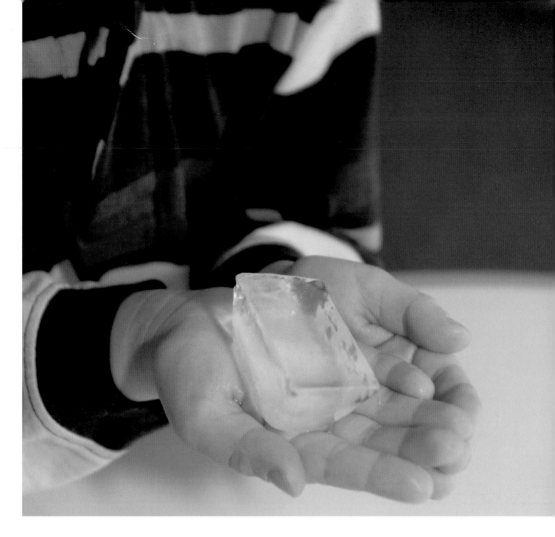

A **solid** is a kind of matter.

A solid has its own shape.

Most solids do not take the shape of their containers.

A rock is a solid.  Solids can be
hard.

A toy is a solid.  Solids can be soft.

A tree is a solid.  Solids can be thick.

A ribbon is a solid. Solids can be thin.

Cutting a solid changes its size.

But it is still a solid.

Heating a solid can change
its shape.

Heat can change a solid into
a **liquid.**

Heat can **melt** wax.

Look around. What solids do you see?

# Dissolving

Some solids dissolve in water. When a solid dissolves in a liquid, it looks like the solid has disappeared.  Actually, the solid has broken into very tiny pieces and mixed with the liquid.  This new liquid is called a solution.  The experiment on the next page is an easy way to see dissolving in action.

Fill an empty tea bag
with red drink mix.

Fill a clear glass
with water.

Put the tea bag in the
water. Do not let it touch
the bottom of the glass.

Look closely at the liquid
under the tea bag. Can
you see any movement?

The tea bag is empty.
The drink mix has
dissolved in the water.
The cup now holds a
drink mix solution.

# Solid Facts

 Some solids, like wood and wax, float in water. Other solids, like most rocks and metal, sink.

 A diamond is the hardest natural solid. People make jewelry with diamonds.

 The softest natural solid is graphite. It is the lead in pencils.

 Some solids, like dry ice, can change directly into a gas. They do not become liquid first.

Solids like dough and soil can take the shape of their containers. These solids need to be squished to change their shapes.

To make a chocolate candy bar, solid chocolate is melted. Then the liquid chocolate is poured into a container called a mold. The chocolate cools and becomes solid again. The solid chocolate keeps its new shape when it is taken out of the mold.

# Glossary

 **liquid** – something that flows

 **matter** – anything that takes up space

 **melt** – to change from a solid to a liquid

 **solid** – something that has a definite shape

# Index

The photographs in this book are used with the permission of: © Erica Johnson/Independent Picture Service, front cover, pp. 7, 14; © Royalty-Free/CORBIS, pp. 2, 6, 10, 22 (second from top); PhotoDisc Royalty Free by Getty Images, pp. 3, 4 (right); © Todd Strand/Independent Picture Service, pp. 4 (top), 5, 11, 12, 13, 22 (bottom); © Ryan McVay/Photodisc Green/Getty Images, p. 4 (bottom); © Brendan Curran/Independent Picture Service, p. 8; © Purestock/ SuperStock, p. 9; © age fotostock/SuperStock, pp. 15, 22 (top); © Photodisc/Photodisc Green/ Getty Images, pp. 16, 22 (second from bottom); USDA Photo, p. 17.

Illustration on page 19 by Laura Westlund/Independent Picture Service

Lerner Publications Company
A division of Lerner Publishing Group
241 First Avenue North
Minneapolis, MN 55401 U.S.A.

Website address: www.lernerbooks.com


Library of Congress Cataloging-in-Publication Data

Boothroyd, Jennifer, 1972–
    What is a solid? / by Jennifer Boothroyd.
      p.   cm. —  (First step nonfiction)
    Includes index.
    ISBN-13: 978–0–8225–6836–0 (lib. bdg. : alk. paper)
    ISBN-10: 0–8225–6836–5 (lib. bdg. : alk. paper)
    1. Solids—Juvenile literature.  2. Solid state physics—Juvenile literature.  I. Title.
  II. Series.
  QC176.3.B66 2007
  530.4'1—dc22                                   2006006307

Manufactured in the United States of America
1 2 3 4 5 6 – DP – 12 11 10 09 08 07